8|4

AMERICAN AMNESIAC

AMERICAN AMNESIAC

Diane Raptosh

etruscan press

Etruscan Press
Wilkes University
84 West South Street
Wilkes-Barre, PA 18766
(570) 408-4546

WILKES UNIVERSITY

www.etruscanpress.org

Published 2013 by Etruscan Press
Printed in the United States of America
Cover art by Robin Selditch
Design by Julianne Popovec
The text of this book is set in Georgia.

First Edition

13 14 15 16 17 5 4 3 2 1

Please turn to the back of this book for a list of the sustaining funders of Etruscan Press.

This book is printed on recycled, acid-free paper.

Dedicated to my daughters, Keats and Colette

AMERICAN
AMNESIAC

Acknowledgments

Grateful acknowledgement is made to the editors of the following journals and anthologies in which some of these poems first appeared: *The Ghazal Page*, "The name *Rinehart* bangs no gongs," "I'm neither too disturbed by my odd fate," "The name's John Doe. And I am a place," "With the name John Doe I can remain the man," and "If pressed to name my brand of worldly thought"; *New Verse News*, "I've started to save the weeks' headlines" (published under the title "World Headlines Western Bastard Ghazal"); *Recursive Angel*, "I can't bear the airlessness of crossword" and "Today's diagnosis has it I've got"; *OccuPoetry*, "We have to tolerate inequality as a way" and "Is it just me or have tales of repression"; *The Newer York*, "I found the following entry in the *Legal*," "*A petition to change the name of Miguel*" and "*A Petition to change the name of Jyotisimita*"; *S/tick*, "The first known use of *John Doe*," "James Brown, by his own admission, was," and "To *lag* is to go slow. To *stray* is"; and *Spiral Orb*, "The largest landfill in the world" and "Today I read about the green sea slug."

Numerous friends, colleagues, and family members provided sustenance—aesthetic and intellectual, technical and nutritional, and many of these people gave their detailed attention to this book. For such kindness I offer profoundest thanks to the following: Rob Carney, Keats Raptosh Conley, Lea Cooper, Randall Couch, Renee E. D'Aoust, Jackie Fowler, Edvige Giunta, Harvey Hix, Maimuna Dali Islam, Peter Jackson, Diane Jarvenpa, Vicki Lindner, Robin Lorentzen, Terry Mazurak, Jerome McGann, Alan Minskoff, Letty Nutt, Kenneth Pedersen, Julianne Popovec, Rhonda Prudhomme, Colette Raptosh, Connie Raptosh, Eric Raptosh, Karen Raptosh, Betty Rodgers, Ken Rodgers, Carla Stern, Catherine Veg, Kerri Webster, and Megan Williams. I extend very special thanks to Lucinda Wong for her unerring eye and superlative work helping to prepare this manuscript.

I am indebted to my wonderful writing students—past and present—for whom I am compelled to write my heart out.

I extend my sincerest thanks to The Banff Centre and The Studios of Key West for writing residencies during which I worked on this book.

Particular thanks go out to the faculty, staff, and administration of The College of Idaho, all of whom help support my writing, yes, but, more importantly, remain committed to the overall importance of literature in a life well lived.

I am especially grateful to everyone at Etruscan Press for their celebration of the role of the imagination as well as their commitment to publishing books that trace, refract and frame the conscience of a culture. I give a special shout-out to Phil Brady, for his bighearted reading of the book in the first place. I thank Starr Troup for her brilliant and tireless work throughout every stage of the book's production.

AMERICAN
AMNESIAC

~~ **I** ~~

The name *Rinehart* bangs no gongs, but, man, this photo does:
the handlebar mustache, that wrecked blond wing slung across the brow.

It's who I think myself to be but please keep calling me John Doe; the name
is calm, a truth, the meaning of itself. It fits me like a velvet movie seat.

I fear someday my recall may come back: Will I want it? Will it want in
like water always does? I sit here reading my own mind, widower to all

but wonder's worn down ear. . . . John Doe AKA *Cal Rinehart:*
Calvin J. Ex sous chef. Favorite recipe: Fort Adams Fried Okra.

Think-tanker in Singapore. Financial consultant. Art historian.
Husband. Apprentice in P.R. NGO pundit. The doctors say I am

my kid sister's sibling (I've lost her name). We had a falling out.
Low winds blew wide all blood-trust at once. I flagged an orange bus

and woke in Civic Center Park three states away, four hundred bucks
stuffed in my right sleeve. My life has always been a flock of mishaps

waiting to take flight. The accident of life works no wonders
for the nervous system. Six docs have ruled out epilepsy and delirium.

I'm neither too disturbed by my odd fate nor merely casual.
I sit here with some bread and syllabub and try to reassemble who I am.

And was. Here, have a sip—sweet cream and wine. It salves the nerves.
This much for sure (I think), I'm from the U.S. How mad would I have to be

to say *He beheld a better order in Ravenna, where he began*
to unbelong from every place he knew? Or better still,

They say it was the broken neck of basic decency he had to flee?
I've had to man my own protectorate, it's true. But worlds are never

quite that willed. The rational mind's the moon we trust—but through it
ululates mirage. No knowing is neutral. Here's how it is:

My name is John Doe. My name is Calvin J. Rinehart.
And I have agnosia. Amnesia. One of the two. Plus four hundred dollars

to both of my names. This large box of files. Somebody's cookware.
I've forgotten what herbs do. Where my bills are. Don't know my mother.

Say, Cal, does the soul have a torso? The self is a smalto. A smart card.
So far as I know, the *I* is another, is a green blazer, a waiter suspended on a tray.

The name's John Doe. And I am a place, the holder of a pose.
        All selves serve as other people, and I'm no exception.

Calvin J. Rinehart must be some fabulist's rendition
        of a different face. Or turn of mind. I'm John, complete

with silent middle *h*. I've heard the docs kvetching in their gowns:
        We're pleased to say we're pretty sure that John—or Cal—is genuine.

I, in turn, wax into what I listen to. Just now a thousand sea chameleons
        chomp down crabs. I see their wide black, bat-shaped pupils.

Their blue-green blood, bubbles of ink acting as decoys. My body
        remembers the sensible objects that used to quiver around it:

my two plastic sacks full of meds, the outpatient papers, those four fat squirrels
        chousing each other up the honey locust. I remember my wife, Lisette,

but friends and loved ones have it that I never married.
        I found her daubed out on our couch when she lost our child.

Since then I've searched for something kind and specific. *Der Tafelspitz
        in den Fleischtöpfen Wiens,* to start. The soul's composed of the entire planet.

5

With the name John Doe I can remain the man on the street
from inside this home. Every face will stay new, including my own.

Each word and sentence too. And every sentience must come to feel secure. . . .
A few things are finally starting to come clear—the long thin bones of rain

help me to think. I have lived in Bratislava, Slovakia. Baked bread
for the homeless in New York. Attended a grade school named Izzie Brown.

Backpacked across New Zealand, where I recently delivered an address.
I have heard of what is thought to be the coldest, calmest

place on earth, where no man has set boot. Australian scientists
call this land *Ridge A,* high on the Antarctic flats, landmass

at the bottom of the world—so calm no wind blows at all.
Its sky is dark and dry. I'd like to go there. But I'm a missing man.

I am a man missing a nation and a wife, strung up between a past
I may not want and a present in which I cannot make myself at ease.

*Cal J. will be fondly recalled as the race's member who could not
remember,* scientists bray into the left ear of the penguin emperor.

If pressed to name my brand of worldly thought, track the words,
I'd call it. . . *Incredulous Bolshevistic Placidity.* Or perhaps

Skeptical Insurrectionary Tranquility. I have to feel what I think
or I can't even finish a sentence. I've had to learn to get by

like folks do after fire takes their house—
how to live without loving stuff: the 11-inch sauté pans' wooden handles,

minus the wedding silver. I am forced to slow
my nervous system almost to

a halt. I crush coriander seeds between heartbeats: mushrooms
à la Grecque. I think. Anonymity allows us to understand

we're always shadowed by our third-string selves.
The six-eyed jumping sand spider has this inborn camouflage technique:

buries itself in beach. I form no new memories—inhumed by the now,
a nightmare waiting to be dreamed about. Coriander is an herb.

I sometimes think I'm slowly coming to. I am participant-observer
of Cal J./J. Doe. At odds and harmonious: an outhouse with two seats.

I've started to save the weeks' headlines:

Melting Arctic Makes Way for Man
Man Pretending to Fall Off Bridge Actually Falls

World Wide Web Means the End of Forgetting
United Nations Affirms Human Right to Blaspheme

Iraq Memo: 'Everyone Knows Someone Killed by the War'
Churchgoers Most Likely to Back Torture

Big Pharma Fouls U.S. Water Supply
Rare Storm Wreaks Havoc like Sideways Tornado

Battling Death, Armies, and One's Own Preoccupations
Lawnmower Saves Man from Exploding Grenade

Russian Steel Plant Tells Workers 'Grow Potatoes Here'
New Frog Species Abound in Madagascar

Couple Detained for Sex on Windsor Castle Lawn
Monkeys Ponder What Could Have Been

My marriage to Lisette: never officially registered. Passport's
expired. My license. My social. My deranged identity works now

like some new mark of feral punctuation~~yet to be regulated.
And I, John Doe, hang on by the handlebars of my moustache~~

a mark of resistance. Please don't call me Rinehart, as I do not
recognize the name. But I'll let him be as much a part of me

as water must. My marriage was hidden from friends and family.
Ours was a wild domesticity: We had to drill a hole in the west corner

of the bathroom floor so when the toilet overflowed, water
could drain to the crawl space below. We didn't own much

till the later years. But our union registered dash and plenitude.
Twice a month we'd slather each other in edible body glitter.

I found her daubed out on our couch, our Kansas apartment. Next thing I know
I'm sprawled on a bench in Civic Center Park staring at striped maples.

I missed a presidential election. *Rinehart's pronounced null~~*
shortly after which, the corporation came to be declared a person.

The corporation, in its artificial skin, has gained rights once granted
     only to natural persons. Am I, John Doe, one of them?

Minoan Crete saw no distinction between plant, animal, or human.
     I haven't touched another person's face in a dog's life.

I cook and watch the Rockies from within this respite home:
     rows of hewn pectorals safeguarding my girth. I want to go

work for UNESCO. I want to work crossword puzzles but can't.
     The channel I'm most comfortable with is in Spanish

because it shows world news. I write down names I remember
     in a notebook: Rip Torn, Kaiser Wilhelm I and II—monikers

friends loaned me ages ago. Bloggers from across the world
     predict *What 'happened' to Cal Rinehart will become widespread*

  if ID cards fall into currency: round-the-globe government-controlled
     DNA database hubs. A mug's game! A blunt kick in the khakis!

Frank Capra cast clean-shaved Gary Cooper as John Doe/Long John Willoughby.
     Lisette always said a full mustache made a face look dirty.

We are all in sales, vending our accomplishments and charms,
insists this book titled <u>2013</u>: *The subtext of each encounter*

includes at least one of the following: 1) *I'm trying to get you*
to believe I am who I say I am, and 2) *I'm trying to make you*

accept that I get what you've been through. My version's
not quite verbatim but even my horoscope claims

I should cease to be so secretive about myself. Maybe it *is* right—
I should shout *hallelujah, I am John Doe!* as I pinch myself

on the haunch, pat myself on the pate, and at the same time
swivel to James Brown and whiff these crimson pirate daylilies.

It's true: I've fallen in omni-directional love these past few weeks.
With this bowl of pluots my nurse brought me. With this mock diagnosis:

Sphenopalatine Ganglioneuralgia. It means *Brain Freeze.* O BFFs
from this unfinished planet, it's such clean joy to curate who I say I'll be.

And I will do this from that wide-slung space—that Kansas—tucked
        between anxiety and ennui. And I will do this through the vehicle

of talk-singing, like Bob Hope in the duet "Thanks
        for the Memory" with Shirley Ross—if this comparison is not

abuse of my frailty. How blank the past feels till I roll out its edges
        like bread dough. I'm a man between states, countries,

and any day now Sheriff Joe Arpaio's going to burst in
        past the nurse's station and ask for my papers. Perhaps

I'm more like Gene Kelly, who felt he had the edge on those who could sing
        since he could talk his way through a song. Sometimes it seems Arpaio

is lip-synching to his own pre-recorded performance,
        over 400 microbial species making a home in his mouth as he rounds up

his immigrants and howls them into tent cities. *The American people need*
        an iron hand, says D. B. Norton in Capra's film. He sneers just like Dick Cheney.

I can't bear the airlessness of crossword cubes, so I'll arrange some clues in neat rows: **ACROSS:** 1. See above. 7. Surgical scar. 12. ". . . so long

____ we both shall live?". 19. Bit of excitement. 23. JAIL OR FINE. 27. Jupiter and Saturn. 30. *Bon ton.* Bro. 49. Is indisposed.

53. "You are mistaken!" 69. Permanent resident alien. 73. French suffix. 74. Going all to pieces. 77. Not superficial. 87. Audacious. 89. Pool surface.

91. *Abulia* is one of these. 94. Noxious atmosphere. **DOWN:** 1. Bedamn. 3. Language from which "loot" comes. 12. Mournful lyrics; cheerful

melody. 14. Team whose logo features a blue jay. 15. Controlled fall. 17. Turn 90 degrees, say. 18. *Molder* means this. 24. Trail. 29. Bergman's role

in *Bells of St. Mary's.* 30. "Is _____ a joke?" 47. "Neither here nor there?". 55. Warren : rabbits :: couch : _____. 61. It's on top of piles. 99. Blow

one's stack. 103. Separate abysses. 106. Leadership org. opposed to the G.O.P. 107. Like Joan of Arc. 111. More like a sloth. 119. Is sick with. 121. Separating machine.

One doctor had me trace a path between two outlines of a five-point star,
one inside the other, while I watched both hand and star in a mirror.
With practice I became quite good but couldn't remember doing it before.
A series of Polaroids in a photo album might sketch a life
but never show it whole. My full past flits like this. The star of the hand's

all a matter of density. Present-tenseness is a look askance, the single proof
there is a universe. I write down what I want to remember
but can't due to this dim sheen in my hippocampus: *Contact with dirt*
always makes living beings happier. . . . Deep space smells like hot metal
and fried steak. . . . Declarative memory logs faces, names, and water running out

through other people's walls. I've started collecting words that correspond
to the forgotten positives: *Evitable. Wieldy. Exorable.* Gentle dictionary, everyone wants

an amnesiac to study. Why not the *hippopotamus amphibious*—outsize river horse,
canine teeth grazing on grass? Seems to forget it's mostly whale. Wholly re-porpoised.

When I lived in Kailua, I heard of a man—a woman?—
who had a name problem. She or he wanted to stop being

Waiaulia Alohi anail ke alaamek kawaipi olanihenoheno Kam Paghmani
and become *Waiaulia Alohi anail ke alaamek kawaipi olanihenoheno Kam.*

Now how on earth did I remember this? Purling those globed vowels aloud
causes my tongue to cramp, my hamstrings to ball up like tangerines

jostled in tight crates on western trade routes. . . . Suddenly I've lost my
thought, my feel for place, the taste inside my head~~fingertips harrumphing

to this pen. So how many machines do *you* have day-to-day relations with?
And my detractors claim that *I* hallucinate: *Who's paying for his stint*

at St. Anthony?. . . . Rinehart raises ratings for the Denver Post!. . . .
Calvin Rinehart: Con artist, perhaps?. . . . Obvious alien abduction LOL.

Off-thread, but can we get some mileage from the fact that his Ravenna firm's
ramrodding multicultural themes?. . . . I think he used to live in Oz. . . .

My name was Cal Rinehart. My name is John Doe. Named after
my father's uncle. Went over the side of a lobster boat, seal in his jaws.

Today I read about the green sea slug: half animal, half plant,
        lips shunted like sheer plumped-out plantains. Stalkless,

they suck innards from algal filaments, green branched gut network
        born to burgle organelles and store them in slug cells.

They've formed of their loneliness fusion, tufted gills meshed
        into leaf bracts, mantle gland latticed with small netted veins,

cerata seeing to it this being can breathe precisely from the place
        of something else. Multi-cellular kingdom crossings: I take notes

on much of what I read so I can spot what I think, slowing my nerve network
        to surcease. Try to find the *you* that's neither yours

nor theirs. I'm somehow them and us: Doe/Rinehart~~even a third body,
        humanly mollusk, echoing through the sensual dark.

File this one under *Readers may know more than we do.*
        More than the police. Our sources. Or the subject of the story himself.

State officials say I abused the system for food and warmth. I did not.
I'm unknown but typical: John Doe. John Q. Public. A regular Joe,

I've lost my job, my wife, my home. My sense of who I am
and look to be. Common man called to become dutiful eunuch. A brand:

Guy Hypothetical, bangs slung low across the brow. Someone to whom
nothing is handed or owed, the world's widower~~ever more on hazard's side

of the class divide. I have heard it's best to house truth's tongues
in a closed mouth but I cannot. I keep on writing down words; scenes

round themselves out straight through my arms.
Lonesomeness likes it in this room but it's not chronic.

Andy Warhol had perspective down wrong: I'm able to see
what I am from an objective and subjective point of view.

I am John Doe. I was Calvin J. Rinehart. I was Lisette's first love,
Mother's young man, man on the street glad to feel so grave and weightless:

Joe Public also just happens to be this new jack musical swing group,
which suits me so much better than these pants.

James Brown, by his own admission, was a vibe, a dance, a freedom
he keyed up for humankind. Vibration is civilization. The mover and shaker

may serve at once as financial advisor, think-tanker, and pundit, gliding
in and out of places that enlist his help. I was such a man, impurely

sure of himself—based on what I see in this résumé: a non-state
actor working for firms, quasi-governmental agencies, and NGOs.

Thanks to all these photographs and notes, I know I toyed with
how to lend a self to the world, regardless of fact or track record.

Rinehart was an idea. Like *money* or *loan,* which cannot exist
because the dollar's made of debt and as such cannot be sustained.

Deposit leads us even further from the truth. Inside my sleeve: four hundred dollars
to both of my names. Here is my wedding ring. Here's to Jane and John Public—

I am your knight, your rook, your shoo-in, sole that grows with your kids' feet:
The name's John Doe. I'm dangerous to the touch as Marie Curie's cookbook.

I'm a man without a past, like so many folks who've been expelled
from their own but dare not detect it. *Shake your head no; nod your head yes.*

There's enough amnesia out there to kill a horse. I'll give you
flawless briefings on how to reach the national library in Paris.

And I could chase the ground for hours about sign and archetype
in the Louis XIVth style, jargon loping and swooping

like lemon leaf veins, though I might switch tongues
suddenly to Italian and jump tracks

to the fall of the Roman Empire.
I'm a houseless, nation-free man,

but I am the people—reason and passion in peace accords.
Go figure: *Citizen Exxon* can buy as much speech as *he she it* can afford.

I attended the Culinary Loft, New York, New York. Listen.
To feed another human being is far more exquisite than eating.

Water has memorized this much: Ex-Citizen Rinehart's a leak
in the black hole at the center of all spiral galaxies.

We have to tolerate inequality as a way to gain prosperity for all,
someone told me Goldman Sachs' Lord Griffiths said

at London's Southwark Church last fall. What kind of sense is this?
I can't remember a thing I did for that firm,

but it says on my C.V. I have advised for them.
A thin cut of wisdom: The kinder you are the stronger

your immune system. And don't forget oysters. Dark meat.
The day's breath of garlic. Carelessness can ruin months of growth.

My old best friend Jen Byers says there's such a job
as being minister of leaves of tea!

If someone were to ask which ancient figure I'd most like to meet,
I'd say the constitution, as it is a living document. Get on the page with me.

I recall the end of Rinehart's last consulting phase
as if it were Lisette's first look.

At each momentous stage of his life, a Sioux Indian earns a new name.
Jumping Badger landed the tag *Sitting Bull* on killing his first bison.

Unfriend was just dubbed word of the year.
The name's John Doe, and I'm just lying doggo here on wheezing earth.

Is it just me or have tales of repression, suffering, and cruelty
disappeared from public memory, slipped out of view

like white deer against a rinse of snow?
People aren't so much persons anymore as they are

war fighters, purchasers, prisoners—shoulders bunched up like shrubs.
You can order cancer cells from a catalogue! Money is speech.

Goldfish have a god-big range of recall, so I've read. I can sum up
watching tops of trees, lying on the bench that day in Civic Center Park.

We need to shut down oil infrastructures, and the tips of leaves don't give
if we do this through lawsuits, boycotts or sabotage. But I'm afraid

of assault. Of stroke. I have no memory of fear itself. A street. A bus shelter.
Fake snowflakes wafting from Dubai. My treatment in Florence

for kidney stones. I've grown more oval than the orange roughy. I ache
on all the bodies of each of my parts. I need to clutch another person's face.

Instead, there's this game called Word Bubble, which promises to flex
the memory and help me to *Live Life to the Youngest*. The nurses love this

sort of thing: *We're going to test your YOU-Q,* they chirrup. The screen
presents a three-letter stem. The directions are these—*Guess:* **che**_____.

I'm supposed to quickly list words that begin with those letters.
I have 60 seconds once I click *play*. I come up with only one: *Che*

Guevara. Which adds up to zip. Score: 0 at the *End of Day 1*.
Day 2 comes a few seconds later. Directions—*Guess:* **bus**_____.

I get distracted by ads in the margins: **Find Out How Old
You Really Are.** *Bustling bushwacker businessmen busted.*

Score: 290. It's tomorrow again, or so claims this wizardry, which feels
more like real time than days do themselves. Which means

I should practice practicing death. Or maybe play chess. Our muscle
memory seems always to make us turn blurred data into debacle.

Visionandpsychosis.net suggests my state is caused by Subliminal
    Distraction exposure. But what the hell is that?

Something to do with psychotic episodes of men in cubicles.
    I beheld a better system in Ravenna, but I didn't stay there.

Maybe they should just lock me up in the Rodin Museum.
    The Schacter Memory Lab. A penitentiary kitchen.

Today I read a new prison opens up each week somewhere in the U.S.
    The last time I was touched, it was a one-armed hug: this stumped young cop

on a Denver sidewalk. But let's change the subject.
    I am the lone caretaker of this electric lime coleus.

I was Calvin J. Rinehart. I am Citizen John Doe,
    agent of the hoi polloi. Created character, I've read, is vital

to keeping order, but the Supreme Court can't find a difference between
    natural citizens and business entities invented by the state. I am The Man

on the Street, John Doe in virtual lockdown~~no criminal bent beyond
    spurting free bits of wisdom. My parents ran a nursing home for aged children.

~~ II ~~

How you say *John Doe* in other languages: In the Philippines
the common man's *Juan de la Cruz*. In Slovenia,

Janez Novak—translated *James of the New*. Italian
equivalent: *Mario Rossi*. Even a cartoon character's named

after him. In Icelandic, John Doe is *John Johnsson*. In Dutch,
Jan Lul, a somewhat derogatory term. In Bangla, *Rahim* or *Karim*.

In Cantonese: *Chan Siu Ming;* Australia: *Fred Nurk,*
as in *'Fraid Not* in a deep Aussie accent. *Joe Farnarkler's* another.

Farnarkler, Aussie wisdom says, is Bullshit Artist. A man who knows me
from Taiwan writes that I'm arrogant, that mine is the *fleshiest prat*

on the fat earth, full of B.S. I'm afraid I'm not. I'm afraid fear
has reordered the world. I continue to organize files into masses of clues.

Looks like Cal is loose, and not in the funny Down Under way, writes an old pal
who, yes, has unfriended me. In Capra's film, John Doe dies for the sake of humanity.

Thinking and speaking and feeling-in-knowing have come to
    eclipse physical strength as paths to success. As has the knack

to sit still and focus. Nurse Roxanne's really good at this. As was
    Lisette. Now Jane Doe's the closest thing I have to *my better half.*

I wish to tip my hat to each of her in every tongue I don't quite know:
    to the Finnish *Maija Meikalainen,* to the Hindi *Anamika,* Nameless One,

and to German's *Erika Mustermann,* which basically means
    Mrs. Exampleman. Americans no longer ask, for instance, of a judicial ruling,

is it right? or *is it just?*, but Erika might well. Better still, run a solemn
    matter past Icelandic *Johna Johnsdottir,* daughter of some average John or Joe.

Might a given act serve the public good? Just ask Serbia's *Ivana
    Ivanovic.* Or try Portugal's *Maria das Couves,* which actually means

Mary of Cabbages. An Italian orphan is sometimes called *Esposito.* It means *exposed.*
    As in *left to the elements.* As in when one's kicked out. On one's sister's gusty doorstep.

I found the following entry in the *Legal Notices Section*

in between the *Music* and the *Kisses* columns and

above the *MegaMates Connection* portion of my local

weekly—one more person's complex rechristening:

A petition to change the name of ZiYi Wong, born

in Tieling, Liaoning, People's Republic of China

has been filed in Glendale, CO. The child's

father is living. The child's mother is

living. The petitioner's name will

change to Prince ZiYi Wong

because the child wants it to

have an English ring.

            Pale males will not have been
the wronged minority, despite what they'll no doubt come to say. Such chants

            will ring far past the Lone Star
State. White men as sum of the electorate are sheets of shrinking sea ice. Notice

            I do not say *we*, as I am more
a lightish shade of pink—for which phrase Procol Harum would probably like to

            throw a shoe at me. Texas has
repeated dreams of breaking itself down to build its face anew. Have you heard

            about the man who couldn't keep
from having total recall? Could not forget a single row of teeth. And he could taste six

            shades of blue. He was nowise a self-
made man. Created character is vital to keeping order. Heidegger said, *What's artful*

            forces being from forgetfulness. Something along these lines. Name's John Doe.
I'm a straight light pink man. I sip hot water from a shot glass as I scan the news.

'Frankenstein' Doc Creates Synth Life
New Pictures Show Jupiter Missing a Stripe

Global Kiss-In: More than Just Lip Service
Privacy Breaches: How to Avoid Making Headlines

Dalai Lama Claims World is Growing Happier
Hair—and Fur—Today, Soaking Up Oil Spills Tomorrow?

'Gringo Masks' Let Nervous Arizonans Whiten Up
Analysis: Two Tables at Israel-Palestine Proximity Talks

Notorious Spelling Mistakes: Famous Mashed Words
Pink Dolphin Photos Leave Photographer Tickled Pink

Old Man Cuffed in Italy for Coke in Oranges
Osprey Loses Carp Lunch to Power Line, Causing Outage

Doomsday Shelters Making Sudden Comeback
Seagull Flies with Crossbow Dart in Head

According to my notes, I've read a lot of depth psychology.
    Synchronicities are slits in the fabric of the day-to-day, swift ruptures

revealing unified orders of mind and matter. I've no idea how
    I got here, or why. If Rinehart was resinous exocarp, I am zest's own

hesperidium—blood orange. Kumquat. A lemon. Good metaphors
    are forces even Homeland Security should worry about. *Pound and cut them*

from the air and from the sea. We've sealed ourselves off
    from systems of wits that simplify us: chemical bonds creating solidity

from near vacant stuff—matter that bends space, brains that produce thought,
    finches evolved to suck the blood of their dead. Fear's re-sorted the universe,

tiny reverse vacuums carpeting Earth in fuchsia-colored dust undetectable
    except in moments of cleanly seeing through. The days are not easily made.

Tonight I'm Inexhaustible Being cloaked in John Doe, who used to masquerade
    as Cal J.~~raw kumquat pleased to serve as your martini garnish.

I want to be all places at once and do everything at the same
time. I guess I'm in luck, since today's horoscope says *No more*

of this linear one-day-at-a-time stuff. I want a whole week shoehorned
into each 24-hour crank of Earth's wheel. Sometimes even as Doe

I want enough money to fill up Lake Tahoe at the same time as I'd like
to live as if there's no such thing as dollar bills. I'd love to chew

thought's cud in the streets, where philosophy started. Herr
Heidegger liked to walk the Black Forest. This makes me fear for my heart.

Even our Freiburg philosopher suffered a wound in his thought:
his attachment to fascism. *Great men make great errors,* he came to

insist. Metaphysicians say things the people do not. In truth
I am the Great Wan Indoorsman. Cookware-hugger. A radiogenic solo act.

Sometimes Lisette sighed words that blurred past all meaning: *People
were meant to be placed in groups. This trait separates them from the rest of humanity. . . .*

is the united states a christian nation

is the united states a corporation

is the united states a demo

is the united states a democracy

is the united states a democratic republic

is the united states a federal republic

is the united states a fedora

is the united states an imp

is the united states an imperialist nation

is the united states in a depression

is the united states a kingdom

is the united kingdom a country

is the united states a nation-state

is the united states a net importer of steel

is the united states on recess

is the united states on the verge of collapse

is the united states the only place that doesn't use the metric system

is the united states the new rome

is the united states wall-eyed

is the united states wall street

is the united states young

is the united states zydeco-friendly to anyone

Ӝ Ӝ Ӝ

Last night I was looking for bean recipes. I forgot how to spell *fagioli*.
The laptop came at me with its unease: *Did you mean: <u>fragile</u>?*

Today's diagnosis: dissociative fugue, a forgetting disease
marked by a purposeful need to leave home—a theme that repeats

through fixed numbers of parts. I remember giving
a slideshow in Greece on the Vienna Secession, emphasis: Gustav

Klimt's bold-eyed Pallas Athena—goddess of causes, wisdom, and the arts.
Capitalist ideology works to craft beings in its image. Sometimes

Lisette and I used to flamenco in our living room. We'd press our foreheads
together to finish, like mouths in a smooch: I could feel the brain in my hips,

lower back connect straight to my fingertips. No tree has leaves so foolish
as to spar among themselves. . . . *During the fugue there's no recall of the former life.*

The beloved dead are our charge. The beleaguered living. Meanwhile the damned
bloggers: *I'll bet this Rinehart must be running for mayor. He doesn't seem to know*

anything about being one and he came out of nowhere—a moose blown out of
the stratosphere. A whack job. Virgin Mary staring from your blurry crepe.

The Athena of myth is paradox: outwardly female, inwardly male.
    In the modern era—emphasis on detachment, passion is thought

quixotic, emotion of a lesser ilk than reason. Athena is the single
    goddess heroes trust: possessed, she seems, of objective wisdom,

born of a man. I came to know Athena through her arms. That helmet.
    The scaly shield or aegis. Her owl as companion. In Klimt's work

her eyes stare clean out of the picture, lips flexed in a thin firm line.
    That vertical posture, matched by the spear, speaks to her strength.

The figure of the nude at bottom left seems out of place. I look
    upon her here: Athena props this tranquil waif, arms outstretched, holding up

a mirror. Men choose at whom to gaze. The woman's curls are aflame,
    her nipples tick upward. The ledge of her chin. She tenders ways to lend herself

to the world. Wisdom and war are mind-mates for our patron goddess.
    Contradictions help create free will. Lisette's beloved lipstick shade was *Fearless*.

There's no mesh to what I know, just as there are so few shades
of grey in public speech: rewards for obedience,

reprimands for veering off the line. . . . I'm searching for
something kind and specific: my frayed day planner, some classic R & B,

my blue ID bracelet. This résumé photo's
definitely me, skin on my chin from an orange rind. Those slow circles of certainty.

Now I'm one of the *sans papiers,* a homeless
asylum seeker managing to attract distaste. We've come to the imperium

forewarned by Washington's farewell
address. I keep a copy of it in my left front pocket. To understand

means to know how to go on, though I've no idea
who said this. *The tongue is a soul.* I wrote this on a sticky note and fixed it to my tube

of Brother's Love Bavarian Moustache Pomade. Which helps set up these savage
handlebars~~in *hazelnut*. You can also get it in *clear*.

William Jennings Bryan would have looked great in a *Zorro.*
Or maybe a *copstash,* stumping the land for free silver,

shaping a grass-roots rep for the cause. The right face hair may
have tightened his run against Taft. We elevate a few people

to hero status and forget the rest. Quick: Do jugs of life
drink at your lips? Does anyone remember Lois Gibbs?

The name banged none of my gongs, but I saved this news clip
from the 1978 *Niagara Gazette,* the year I met

my wife. Gibbs organized the neighborhood of Love
Canal and later formed the Citizens' Clearinghouse

for Hazardous Waste. Truth is, early on, Frank Zappa couldn't afford
session horn players. Most of the moisture's blown out of my fingertips.

This makes it hard to turn the page about life
with Lisette. Nights, I plunge my fingerpads in aromatic wax and let them steep.

The public finally urged Bryan to ditch silver and muse
      on imperialism. Business trusts. Bryan was more like a giant

bowl of risotto than a great idea. *Is John Doe trying to put one*
      over on you?, blogger Hank Ray wants to know. Is risotto a form

of rice or pasta? Bryan's famous phrase was *You shall not*
      crucify mankind upon a cross of gold. The world's become a church

of firms, the nations of the world its acronyms: ITT,
      IBM, AT&T, all unease drugged, all boredoms granted

screens to watch—meals brought to you by Corn Syrup—citizens made to serve
      a common profit. A good risotto's barley: It should ooze onto the plate like flows

of lava. Blue Earth's most talky blogger maintains *Rinehart looks like a cross*
      between Nigel Bruce and the black and white Monopoly Man straight from the game.

ITT can mean *It's Time To* and *Invitation To Tender.* What's not to love? *In This Thread,*
      Sir Blogman asks *Who has amnesia here? Cal Rinehart? Cops and docs? The rest of us?*

Thomas Hardy. Joseph Stalin. Bertrand Russell. Dali. Rollie Fingers.
Frederic Nietzsche. Hulk Hogan. Frank Zappa. Goose Gossage.

Archduke Ferdinand. Dick Dastardly. These gents have in common what?
Hairy appendage on the top lip. With graspable stray ends. Sacco's sideman

Vanzetti could almost grab his. There is some grey area as to which
'stache is and isn't *handlebar*. One might also have cause to ask

Is the kazoo an instrument? And *who is really who?* With *handlebar,*
whiskers droop over the mouth, admired by men of every economic

status: the Gilded Age's *bon vivant* Chet Arthur all the way to Captain
Kangaroo. Carelessness can ruin months of growth. For a spell

I sported the *mouthbrow,* which I penciled to a deep red-gold. Much later,
the *horseshoe*. Dragged the jowls down. Rinehart~~in his imperial 'bars~~

must wonder if anyone's missing him. I, John Doe, thumb these slim strands of despair.
In his album *Freak Out!* Zappa blew a green kazoo to lend some comic feel.

Rev Up Your Recall Playing Wordsearch. Today's Theme: **Get and Give.**

```
b  f  q  m  e  r  u  t  p  a  c
d  s  c  x  d  d  o  n  a  t  e
p  i  l  f  e  r  i  u  q  c  a
h  a  u  l  y  z  g  b  i  p  u
c  o  m  m  i  t  j  x  c  u  g
r  s  y  r  e  f  s  n  a  r  t
a  n  r  v  m  t  t  u  t  l  p
e  g  c  h  e  b  e  s  t  o  w
s  o  i  a  r  e  c  l  a  i  m
z  f  l  e  p  u  g  i  d  n  t
t  r  a  p  m  i  b  e  k  a  t
```

I don't like underlining at diagonals. Or verticals. I thus leave

lift, purloin, search, and *steal* for someone else to find.

The first known use of *John Doe:* England, 1659:
To prosecute the suit, to witt John Doe and Richard Roe.

May go back as far as King Edward III. This means
the search for objectivity describes *the Universal Man*

as some guy straight from the land of bangers and mash. Or Cambridge,
Mass. While I digress, neutrality's bias carries vitamin water

for the power elite. Facts watch themselves in the hippocampus: I'm sure
you've heard this all before, to wit I am John Doe, and pale American

males are pretty much seething. I'm light as shorn wheat. I glint a damp
tinge of pink. I've no sense of who I'm supposed to be. But I'm o.k. with it.

I buy the jujubes I used to eat during years that I blank on. Tickles
the limbic system. I write down most of what I read. And underline what's left.

New memories spring from these acts. And lemon-scent sting. What you are not is
half of what you are: This guy who claims he has his PhD in *game* has just friended me

When I was searching the Web for a place I could practice
analogies, this giant red product pulsed forth its promise to **Let You**

Take Control of Your Identity. Would that it could be so easy!
Still, finding the right word-parallels helps tighten memory.

Those boxes of matched words take me back to days working in cubicles,
so I have to retype them, rows of clean seeds. Here is the kernel analogy:

UPBRAID : REPROACH :: I have to choose among *(A) Dote : Like.*
(B) Lag : Stray. (C) Vex : Please. (D) Earn : Desire. (E) Recast : Explain.

Explanation: The correct answer is option A because. . . . I thought it was
E, since *recast* I think means *to reshape more strongly*. But that is beside

the point. I admire how word duos like *dote* and *like* take up houses
next door, like a married couple that needs lots of privacy~~glad of their likeness,

at ease with polarities, pleased to have different front doors. For now, I'll just find
some new pairs that might like to shack up: *divine : dispel, beachhead : riffle, recovery : cure.*

The largest landfill in the world floats within the ocean's midriff: a slowly moving
    clockwise current-spiral sparked

and girdled by high-pressure systems of air. Unnatural wonder of the water-world
    in the neighborhood of the horse

latitudes: the Great Pacific Garbage Patch, twice the size of Texas-and-two-thirds.
    This vortex captures millions of pounds

of trash from around the world. Pelagic plastics dervish-dance with phytoplankton;
    fishermen drag in deflated green

balloons, strings still attached. Confetti krill can't help but choke on tiny resin
    pellets known as *nurdles* while the garbage gyre

stockpiles noxious flecks invisible to the naked eye. I sometimes see the unseen
    clearer than paths no longer

mine. People from across the world came forth to name me. Time gives whatever
    goes by shape: Lisette's cowlick. A funnel cake. That boot-tip off the sloop of Texas.

Today I am alone with half of me,
the region I am not. Cal Rinehart is this plump mustachio who strides out

across my dread folder in Italian lace-ups.
His skin's a darker shade of pink than even mine. This matters not a whit.

The details of his life do not
sync up, but I'll let him be as much a part of me as water must. You've got to

hear me out on this: Anywhere you
put the needle down in the U.S., you find black musical roots. And before I space it,

Wall Street's rise can thank the cotton trade:
It's not how lost a thing forgotten is but how found we want it to be. Two small, true-

lipped monsters circle my left brow by day. Some
fragments simply drop down to me. The Tibetan word for body: *lu*. This brings to mind

luggage. Lugsail. The body as *lumpfish.* As *blunderbuss*
cutting a rug to someone's old eight-track, rigged to play *Louie   Louie   Louie* nonstop

I am no stander above men and women, but I was
back when. What Rinehart assumed, I won't necessarily assume.

I am John Doe, no more modest than immodest. Whatever
is done to someone else comes back to me. I shake

my bangs equally at bombs and greed. But get a load of this: *Gazump*
is a process by which a price of land is raised higher

than the cost agreed on days before both parties sign their John
Hancocks. Through me surges much about the state of what is,

despite—or due to—amnesia. Prosopagnosia. Fugue.
Whatever this is. I can't recall a thing I did for Sachs. I've forgotten

what herbs do. I don't know my brother. I do not recognize
a world in which the claws of leopard crabs have turned

to oil clubs and flounder swim across the surface of the sea. Sticky
note to anyone who reads: *Does anyone remember Lois Gibbs?*

Does a fifth taste bud lead us to seaweed broth?
      Can a culture survive treating oil like filth?

Do wise men keep their money in a roll?
      Does the soul have a torso?

Is processed meat better for you than pure steak?
      Could my average looks and bushy 'stache cost me my trade?

Would leaders in early 1700s-America have foreseen revolution?
      Should I research old time root-stevedoring as a career option?

If *Willy Pete* is another name for White Phosphorous, what is
      Willy Peter's Cave of Oolong Simplicity, which I found on the net?

Isn't solitude the sole cure for *unfriendedness*?
      Why the doily beneath my electric lime coleus?

Do *recite* and *resist* often sip coffee together?
      Did I forget to salute the mint everywhere?

~~III~~

My name was Calvin J. Rinehart. My name is John
Doe. Which doesn't account for my lack of passport

or wallet. The loss of my wife. Even now when I sit at a table
with objects on top, I'm afraid to break through and touch them.

When new words come to mind, I jot them in green. I whisper these
to myself: *screw pine, blergh, mnemonist.* I get lost when I go for walks.

I try to strengthen my recall staring through candle-flame. I like to sing
along with the Rondells even when I can't get all the words. That Russian

man who couldn't *not* remember everything he did could never build
a story of his world. For him *leffel,* the Yiddish term for *spoon,* was braided

like *challah* itself so hard a word he had to snap it off. Eighteen-
eighties France saw in its indoor workers swells of amnesia and flight: shopkeepers,

clerks, and artisans. Does the past have a future? Amnesiacs can only ever add to who
they'd like to become. That windowsill's a bass line, pulse, a psalm. You may hum along,

For the Russian mnemonist simply called *S*, the number
6 had a whitish hue, while 8 had rills of golden hair, salty

as brine. A synaesthete like Scriabin, *S* would see fireworks
edged in pink hues as he heard tones pitched to high frequencies.

In the 17ᵗʰ century, *pink* was also used to say *yellowish tints*.
To be led by people of brown pigment makes certain white folks

see red. I'm a straight, light rose-colored man plumped up on
far too much Bisphenol-A. Belly pitched across belted slacks, I *am*

the people. If I had to name what we tasted like, it would be sweet
and sour borscht. I sometimes slip a word in a crack of the respite home gate:

Outlaw. Beet root. Citizen. They change shape as I walk by, like mythic coyotes.
Like corn. *Idiot memories* are those memory alone calls forth. One of them moans

about Rinehart: *What a crumbly grey voice he used to have.* Borscht may be purple-red,
orange-pink or green. And cold or hot. Scriabin says the key of major D is golden brown.

Scriabin had a face like a honey cake, handlebar 'stache hung
       on the lower quadrant — lank body a hand in a sleeve lowering

slowly to pour milk. Eyes a bright haze, at least in his photos.
       His hands could barely grasp a ninth. It's said he'd had tics, that

he could not sit still. His color scheme aligned with the circle of fifths.
       To *jog* something means to give it a sharp whisk. Then there's the way

to memorize shades of the rainbow: *Richard of York Gave Battle*
       in Vain: Red, Orange, Yellow, Green, Blue, Indigo, Violet. I used to run

a lap around the home to try and strengthen my brain. But it makes this
       sharp red light rise from my neck. I'd rather sit at my desk and sift clues:

In 1892 Scriabin wrote an E minor fugue. His full name: Alexander
       "Sasha" Scriabin. Of Moscow. Born on Christmas day, according to the Julian

Calendar. *I myself am God*, he'd scratched in one of his journals. *I was Cal J.,*
       now I'm John Doe, I sing to mute ensembles decked with stoop-backed children.

A Petition to change the name of Miguel Vasquez,

born October 6th, 1994, in Guadalajara, Jalisco,

Mexico, residing at 4891 W. Zach Place,

Glendale, CO, has been filed in district court.

The name will change to Michael Miguel

Vasquez, because he has only a first name

and wants to have a first and middle name.

The child's father is living. The child's

mother is living. A hearing on the petition

is scheduled for 1:30 p.m. on August 16th

at the County Courthouse. Objections

may be filed by any person who can

show the court a good reason for this

boy not to gain a new first name.

I don't know who I'm supposed to be has a nice ring to it. We can't
ask what we are without asking when, within which mixes,

how weighted, who's strung up in *we*. Bearing the name John Doe
is sure to cause hardships with airport security: This makes me

one more brand of hobgoblin: Marauding Everyman! Domestic
invader—person as purple loosestrife: Ransack his gear! I am o.k.

with this, as I'm still the people. And I'm done with the clench
of a listening which always knows what will come next. Done

bowing to baubles only the I-person wants, skin thin as kiwi sheath.
As far back as I can remember, the *I*'s been another, been a loose blazer.

We must become *them* even if *they* means these bloggers: *After all
this city did for him, he forgets us completely—as well as our parks,*

*our hospitals, our social workers This guy smells about as genuine
as Balloon Boy. Perhaps he should have spent his last 400 bucks at Hempfest.*

xx

If you shave off his chardonnay filter trap, he looks like Mayor McLiberal:
That Oregon socialist-expose-yourself-to-art guy looked like this schmuck's twin!

**

He's a guy wandering the woods. Doesn't know who he is. How's this
a liberal vs. conservative spat? Blast that chew out of your lower lip!

**

Whoosh, buddy, what's that flying right over your head? Heh. Lay down
your brie and box wine and brush the baguette crumbs from your beard.

**

I think he ended up in one of the more compassionate towns in the U.S. BTW,
I had a friend come down with this forgetting thing. Faked the whole shebang.

**

Town's a hellhole far as compassion goes. You seen the lines outside
the shelters? Schools made of paper. Paper made outta elephant shit.

**

Oh, and did you check the bit about his "notebook"—all the clippings
he collects about stuff. A vag. A shamateur. Plainly angling for a book deal.

**

& I still want to know how his wife died. I ask because he wouldn't be the first to take
it on the lam and fake amnesia. & don't go dragging some pinched god into all this.

**

O but nevermind. All you fetus worshippers would run to his aid if
he was in the womb. Now that he's grown, he means zippo to you.

**

Dude's a white guy. Head to Colfax Ave. Dozens of brothers there
can't remember their names. And they ain't hidin no bank up their sleeve.

**

The Post should do more stories about the "colorful" people on bus 7.
Why would a major paper use the word "colorful" to describe a populace?

**

He's a public relations success. Meantime, the everyday Jose y Juana
have to go to work—if they still have a job. Where's the stories about them?

**

They should look into the psycho-active effects of anti-malarial
inoculations. Especially since this man's spun around the world.

**

Subliminal distraction did not cause his mental break. The cubicle was
designed to stem the vision-startle reflex. That syndrome ends in 1968.

**

If Mr. Rinehart is seeking a life to return to, he is welcome to have mine.
. . . I <3 John Doe but bet my life he'll be found dead inside a year

**

Everyone Knows Someone Killed by the War. In this case, Iraq.
In my case, Roxanne's husband George. Operation Funnel

Unlimited Cash to Killing (OFUCK): brought to you by
the global white-collar criminal class. Which hooks us

on fear. On high fructose syrups. I write down what I
want to remember but can't. I write what I'd almost

rather forget: America peers at itself and sees Citizen
Moolah mic'd with kazoos. I made it on the network

news seven times in one day, along with the phrase
a perfect storm. Somewhere between thinking

and feeling, sensing and knowing, one starts
to transform. O Someone! They just dubbed a

hurricane *Calvin*. Can anyone think of a cragged
fluid word that means *ways of talking to women?*

I thank my nurse for each kind turn. *Thanks for the peach slice,*
Roxanne. Tiny right acts are our finest entitlements. Behind each

plucked fruit lies a hand, like one you might glimpse in the hem
of a Xerox. Daniel Ellsberg, vexed by what phrases like *national*

security and *commander in chief* could be tortured to mean,
copied the Pentagon Papers: 7,000 sheets. Helped by his kids.

He listened like a horse's eye within that lecture hall, 1969,
to speeches draft resisters inked in with their lives. What then?

He found a men's room, kneeled on its floor, and shaved off his
earliest certainties. I made copies of the June 13th *New York Times.*

It was 1971. It was when I smoked Prince Albert in a can. Lately
I've had to ask myself *for whom shall I trim back my moustache?* And *how*

shall I presume? And *do I dare disturb Vietnamistan?* Wind blows the water
white and black. Food ads neither hem nor haw. We blank on why we bother to hang on.

I was my mother's mother, and her mother before that. *If need*
is the mother of invention, who is the mother of need?,

Lichtenberg asked. And who, the *sister of industry?* Low
winds blew wide all blood-trust. In the city, unmothered

Athena sprang from her father's brow. Now I speak pretty
much solely to mythical women. So too, to Roxanne. She grins

with the bridge of her nose, her eyebrows question marks.
I crush coriander seeds with my own heartbeat, cut open clean

rows of them wholly for symmetry. Music listens to us.
My nation is this bundle on my cot. Along with these notes.

My home with Lisette had lines of thin windows. Roxanne's legs
rub each other like exultant horses. She draws from them all

the days of her of her past. I look at my hands as though from the roof
of this respite home. Rinehart always likes to approach right through that corridor.

Cal's the one I used to call Myself: He was me when I plumped
for Goldman Sachs. I've made myself free of the home in his body.

But where might I last? John Doe is a scope, a crypt, a safe with great
legroom. Sometimes if I put a word in a dark place I have trouble seeing it

as I go by. *America* is one such term. It contains *acre* and *cream,*
acme and *ma, crime* and *me.* America has a mashed *car* in it. Each of us

helps corrupt our age. There are 200 times more inmates in this Acme
of Acres than all the stars visible to the naked eye. I underlined this

in green in a library book. I couldn't make myself stop. Marauding
Everyman! Take back his ink pens! His Brother's Love Bavarian wax

may contain flammables! So what kind of country willfully breeds
a permanent black undercaste? Since when did greed wax into brass

self-righteousness? And before I forget: Will the White House live-in grandma
get a chance to say her piece among the echo roses and the floribunda?

If memory is ruptured, one can go on. As long as thinking's not cut off,
we keep a grip on what's possible. Details

on Rinehart pull in through the holes. Besides that moustache,
he had a frown on his forehead,

a bellybutton in his chin, and an elbow bone rose
and fell in his throat. You can't quite see these things in his photos. Thanks

to living in this fugue state, I must wrestle tensions of my own
biography. Being widowed to myself makes me

preside over what yank and fret I have and leave
the rest to, say, Maria of the Cabbages. To Athena. To my nurse

Roxanne. It's a cinch to feel right and wrong plumb in the body.
The rich are richer than at any time in living memory, I read today. What a funny phrase.

What's the window on a Green New Deal? Oh where's my lapel pin?
Do I dare to vex a war? What the hell's the shelf life for collective recall?

Across: 18. Not quite mega-. 26. Supermax resident. 33. Seeing red. 35. Guy. 44. Balloonist's basket. 48. Fund-raising group. 51. Tijuana *that.*

54. Some poetic feet. 59. "Hair" song with the lyric *the air, the air.* 66. Out of concern for. 67. Little argument. 70. Accusatory words.

72. Getting up there in years. 84. Admonishment. 123. Standing need. **DOWN:** 2. With a smile. 3. Not ecclesiastical. 5. Speaker's spot. 7. Give someone

the pheasant eye. 14. Being punished military style. 18. Deep-sea animal. 26. Very sorry. 29. Others. 33. Prisons : crime :: greenhouses : _____.

39. Noted period. 40. Used as a resource. 58. Seeing everything. 63. Fertilizer ingredient. 69. Claim in a cigarette ad. 74. Rash soother.

86. Skin-feeding newt. 90. What the singer cannot hear. 95. Monopoly token. 100. Piece of improvisatory classical music. 101. Fallen nude.

105. Whistle. 111. Sign. 114. To do. 115. XXX x X. 118. Letters in an old box. 120. Vivacious person. 122. Smooched noisily. 129. Gets by slowly.

Schoenberg suggested we hear even the simplest tune
with only the mind's ear, given that our grasp of song

depends on calling on what's gone before and matching it
with what comes next: This I can't do. What has been

cogently thought could soon become a chorus. It might
become a means of never saying *uncle*. Gray winds blow

and my room in this home cracks its masked knuckles.
I've survived my own extinction, like a freak marine

reptile. I have to feel what I think or I can't find who
I want to become. I wax into what I listen to~~into what I underscore.

This could make me someone finer than myself by half, which brings us
to the Ninth Symphony in which Beethoven silently transcends himself as well

as all musics before and since. Where were we a moment ago? Will you wait
here as I mend my vest? Might you help me get mic'd for this signature couplet?

To *lag* is to go slow. To *stray* is to lose one's way.
Going too slowly isn't a stronger form of wandering from one's way.

A yogini told me that with repetition all things honest come:
Bon ami. Calm. Fort Adams fried okra. But it doesn't feel that way.

Explanation: I've yet to hear this lesson from my own mind.
Blurs, blind spots, and memory wounds get in the way.

She also told me if you want to earn someone's respect,
placing your belly button parallel with hers is the best way.

She knew how to make her bones graze the air, her shoulder blades
slide down almost to her hips. This is another way

of saying she knew how to give each moment her entire life.
I'm trying to get there. I'm trying to see if there's a way

to bring together all gradations of John Doe
like a huge portmanteau word there might even be a way to pronounce.

The self is a thousand localities
       like a small nation—assembly required: borders and roads,

armies, farms, small and large pieces of parchment. I stand by
       all the territories I have ever been, even as I can't

remember them. I am a locum—ear to the emperor penguin, a banner ad
       blinking to the hoi polloi. Since I've become John Doe, I swear

I can feel most objects with sixty digits
       instead of five. This makes me think

of Lisette. Makes me miss her left collar bone. Her hips' wingtips.
       A train moans from a far hummock.

Which reminds me that everyone I'll have to live without
       I must help to find a place within. Which is an act

of granite will. A strain. A ditty.
       An exercise in utmost *beautility*.

Roxanne likes to call me *Honey*. Sometimes I call myself
that too. When I flash back to the years sitting at my desk

at the firm, my hands start to shake. *It will be o.k., Honey,*
I say to myself, my own tiny nurse. Why are so many

work stations shaped like Sudoku? Why did
America take the cows off the grass? I'm having trouble

keeping my focus. *Transient Global Amnesia*'s the latest
layover name for what I have. Sounds bohemian. International.

Episodes are usually short-lived~~Honey. A *cure* doesn't work
against *recovery*. I had to take a step back

from time, to leave my own body
though here it is, hanging from itself—a medieval sock hat, stomach

agurgle and rumbling. *Borborygmi* is the living word for that.
Fortuitous : accidental. Reckless : threatening. Cataclysmic : doomed.

Is it possible to let the sleeping life seep into day~~
that bright murk of softness, state of being reverently

at rest yet wide-eyed as Athena's wired owl? Often
when my alarm goes off in the morning, something

alarming happens in my dreams. A pair of words
might land on my face—*Exist : exit. Warren : rabbits.*

Language : anguish. I just read about a scientist
who said humans have so transformed the planet

we should no longer refer to it as *Earth.* We seem on
our way to a very different word. He suggests *Eaarth.*

But what about *Achates,* as in *ancient trusty friend?*
Or how about Planet *Greige,* from the French for *raw,*

unfinished, usually said of silk. But we'll make the word mean
as we see fit: *Heart's wife. Furl of green-blue. A tired outburst of silence.*

A Petition to change the name of Jyotismita Ranjan,

born in Chindar, Maharashtra, India, residing in

Glendale, CO, has been filed in district court.

The name will change to Johlea Mayekar

because the old name is not a balanced

name, but the new one will be. It will

have a stronger intrinsic quality, as

mentioned in the balanced name report.

The petitioner's father has died, and the names

and addresses of the closest blood

relatives are: No one is alive.

The petitioner's mother has died

and the names and addresses

of the closest blood relatives are:

No one is alive.

This morning for the first time in years, the Declaration
        of Independence was loosed from its oxy-free safe. It was

revealed that Jefferson initially referred to American
        people as *subjects*. Then, in an eighteenth-century

version of search-and-replace, he swapped in *citizens*.
        He rethought nation-nature in splendiferous detail.

Accident : fortuitous. Daydreaming may have even helped.
        Quick: Flash onto these four words: *Eye. Gown. Basket.*

Whistle. Can you think of a word that relates to them all?
        Does this have anything to do with *cloud computing? Did you*

mean: fragile? Now I'm just talking to calm myself. At times
        I must breathe my way back into being from the spine in my belly.

I'm afraid fear's realigned Planet *Greige*. We've got a case
        on our hands, Calvin J., task-unrelated :: You've been rephrased.

Maybe nation-nature's now a thing of the past,
state-as-structure eddying down the drain basket.

Maybe the new prototype is open space—Kansas-shape,
or is simply that state of readiness which is ourselves

as we step into a dinner theater: self-releasing
and open sourced, waiters upending their trays

as a means to serve something up-to-the-minute:
jellied drinks and libidinous empathy with a side

of edible chess pieces—memories stored solely
as molecular arrays. I think it was Emerson said

We estimate a man by how much he remembers.
In place of which I'd dish up the following:

We remember a man by how much he esteems the 'we.'
Reasons for our shared forgetting may be found on your television.

Instead of choosing *John Doe,* maybe I should have gone global,
chosen more syllables. Could have said *Call me Anamika,*

whose meanings suggest someone comely, whose name is
unknown. *Anamika* hints at something like this: *The person's*

destiny must not be fixed by a name's denotations.
Anamika can also mean *mighty ring finger.* Mean *little sister.*

Some cultures avoided the true names of powerful entities
and hailed them obliquely. Or labeled them *Nameless.*

Here is *Anamika* in Morse Code: . -- .. . --- .. - . - . - :
Here is my wedding ring; here, a bouquet of vowels: *Anamika,*

spine of a possible decency, whose sounds yield great notions.
Anamika is a field of thinking-in-feeling, the weight of one man's

trials. Of someone's hand upon nation-state. A way to sit still.
And listen. *May I come to know a bit about you for my files?*

A Note on Diane raptosh

Diane Raptosh is the author of three previous poetry collections:
Just West of Now, Labor Songs, and *Parents from a Different
Alphabet.* The recipient of three fellowships in literature from
the Idaho Commission on the Arts, she is the Boise Poet Laureate
(2013) and the Idaho Writer in Residence (2013–2016). She holds
the Eyck-Berringer Endowed Chair in English at The College of
Idaho, where she teaches literature and creative writing as well as
directs the program in criminal justice/prison studies. She lives with
her family in Boise.

Books from Etruscan Press

Zarathustra Must Die | Dorian Alexander
The Disappearance of Seth | Kazim Ali
Drift Ice | Jennifer Atkinson
Crow Man | Tom Bailey
Coronology | Claire Bateman
What We Ask of Flesh | Remica L. Bingham
No Hurry | Michael Blumenthal
Choir of the Wells | Bruce Bond
Cinder | Bruce Bond
Peal | Bruce Bond
Toucans in the Arctic | Scott Coffel
Body of a Dancer | Renée E. D'Aoust
Nahoonkara | Peter Grandbois
Confessions of Doc Williams & Other Poems | William Heyen
The Football Corporations | William Heyen
A Poetics of Hiroshima | William Heyen
Shoah Train | William Heyen
September 11, 2001, American Writers Respond | Edited by William Heyen
As Easy As Lying | H. L. Hix
Chromatic | H. L. Hix
First Fire, Then Birds | H. L. Hix
God Bless | H. L. Hix
Incident Light | H. L. Hix
Legible Heavens | H. L. Hix
Lines of Inquiry | H. L. Hix
Shadows of Houses | H. L. Hix
Wild and Whirling Words: A Poetic Conversation | Moderated by H. L. Hix
Art Into Life | Frederick R. Karl
Free Concert: New and Selected Poems | Milton Kessler
Parallel Lives | Michael Lind
The Burning House | Paul Lisicky
Synergos | Roberto Manzano

Etruscan Press Is Proud of Support Received From

Wilkes University

Youngstown State University

The Raymond John Wean Foundation

The Ohio Arts Council

The Stephen & Jeryl Oristaglio Foundation

The Nathalie & James Andrews Foundation

The National Endowment for the Arts

The Ruth H. Beecher Foundation

The Bates-Manzano Fund

The New Mexico Community Foundation

The Gratia Murphy Endowment

Founded in 2001 with a generous grant from the Oristaglio Foundation, Etruscan Press is a nonprofit cooperative of poets and writers working to produce and promote books that nurture the dialogue among genres, achieve a distinctive voice, and reshape the literary and cultural histories of which we are a part.

etruscan press
www.etruscanpress.org

Etruscan Press books may be ordered from

Consortium Book Sales and Distribution
800.283.3572
www.cbsd.com

Small Press Distribution
800.869.7553
www.spdbooks.org

Etruscan Press is a 501(c)(3) nonprofit organization.
Contributions to Etruscan Press are tax deductible
as allowed under applicable law.
For more information, a prospectus,
or to order one of our titles,
contact us at books@etruscanpress.org.